Antonio Raimondi
Rocco Raimondi

Robert De Niro
and
the Vietnam War

Antonio Raimondi
Rocco Raimondi

"Robert De Niro and the Vietnam War"

Vol. 2
Series of books: «About the Vietnam War»
ISBN   9798590066575

Italy, 2021

INDEX

To those who fought
and those who sacrificed their lives,
To those who wept
and those who waited,
Because of the Vietnam War.

I think the conflict was wrong but what bothered me most was seeing that whoever went to war became a victim of it; soldiers were used for the whims of others. I didn't agree with the decisions of the politicians and what they were doing. It was the right of many to say: "Why do I have to go, get involved in something that is not clear and pay for it with my life?". (Robert De Niro about the Vietnam War)

Robert De Niro, who has always been sensitive to the personal conflicts that troubled veterans and hindered, even many years after the end of the war, their resumption of a normal life, in *Taxi Driver* and *The Deer Hunter* (also in *Jacknife*), has provided his very personal contribution to the Vietnam War Movies through truly extraordinary interpretations that have contributed to increasing the myth of a fundamental actor in the history of cinema.

De Niro is configured as an actor unrelated to classic Hollywood schemes not only for the style of his acting or because he is an antidivo par excellence who hates the clamor of worldliness, but also, and above all, because he is an independent actor who never has bent to the "star-system", he never signed contracts that would have linked him, according to the logic of the Hollywood "studios", to a cinematographic image with well-defined clichés. The image that De Niro offers on the screen is always different with each film.

And his independence from Hollywood even spurred him to establish a film center in New York in 1989, the TriBeCa Film Center, that allows him to better control his career, as he is freer in the evaluation and implementation of film projects.

Even his characters are anti-Hollywood as they are antithetical to the old models of the hero who is the arbiter of his own destiny who, by actively intervening, manages to transform events to his advantage.

De Niro's characters are almost always losers, unable to change their destiny, if not irreversibly ill or hopelessly lonely, even when they are part of a gang or an ethnic community (the mafia, the Italian-Americans, the Slavs). The actor, in choosing his roles, is attracted to contradictory characters: from the good ones who don't always do respectable deeds or from the bad guys who, despite their wickedness, are not entirely incapable of good sentiments.

If I see a person on the street who has some weirdness, some eccentricity, I immediately think it might be interesting to put them in the film: it could be right for the character. Or I can think of images of people I know or have seen, and then I start working on these details.

The qualities of an actor must be those which, according to Faulkner, belong to writers: experience, observation, imagination.

Preparing for a role, working in a film are difficult experiences. When you are ten you dream of beauty, glory and you don't know that reality is above all study and work. While a film is being prepared, the rest of the world disappears: there is no other commitment. (Robert De Niro)

The controlled and stylized classic Hollywood-style acting is far from that of De Niro, who is spontaneous, versatile and prone to improvisation. His preparation to immerse himself in a role is based both on a meticulous analysis of the psyche of the character that he must interpret, and on the observation of external details. According to De Niro, the effective collaboration between director and actors is fundamental, one of the most relevant aspects for the success of a film: it is very important that on the set you can exchange ideas, suggestions and advice.

Moreover, it was often the instinct that suggested to De Niro to improvise many scenes in some of his most famous films, especially in those directed by Martin Scorsese, a director who has always allowed him to express himself with great freedom and with whom he gave life to what is considered one of the most solid and profitable collaborations in the history of cinema. To those who ask him if the common Italian roots have influenced his friendship with the director, Robert replies: «I don't know, I think it's something more profound. Above all, there is the same understanding of things. It was our two personalities, our temperaments that allowed this relationship. Despite Little Italy and everything else, we come from very different backgrounds, yet we met the same.

I can say one thing: Marty is not afraid to experiment. When I tell him: "Listen, it could be done like this...", he listens to me not to please me, but because he really thinks that new ways can be found». Scorsese is in turn grateful to De Niro precisely because the actor has often encouraged him to experiment.

What matters to me is to work with a director who has the same interests as me. The important thing in our work, which is very hard, is to establish complicity and at least a minimum of fun that avoids migraines. (Robert De Niro)

The actor also collaborated with Scorsese in the drafting of some screenplays, restructuring, at times, the most difficult scenes.

De Niro seems to embody better than any other actor the spontaneous and impulsive characters that Scorsese brings to the screen and his improvisations are particularly appreciated by the director who, not infrequently, records and inserts them into the screenplay. During the collaboration, the De Niro/Scorsese duo experienced evolutions of issues dear to both, such as the psychosis produced by urban alienation, life dominated by violence and revenge, the impossibility of maintaining lasting relationships by individuals aimed at affirming their virility.

The characters in Scorsese's films, who have the face of De Niro on the screen, in fact, are all overwhelmed by their obsessions, by their loneliness, by the lack of control over themselves, by the inability to dominate events and communicate with others. Their internal anger and their long-suppressed frustrations suddenly explode in scenes of violence whose brutality has often been a source of disturbance and controversy. For example in *Taxi Driver*, Travis Bickle, a Vietnam veteran who is a taxi driver and wanders the streets of New York, unable to communicate with others and have good relationships with the opposite sex, desperately alone, immersed and trapped in this closed and dark universe of paranoia, perversion and violence, is an extremely enigmatic figure who cannot be fully understood even from his tragic, last gesture. De Niro himself, when asked to explain this character, was unable to give a convincing answer: "I am always asked to explain some scenes but there are things that cannot be explained. I try to play a role from my point of view, but I can't understand why the character does a certain action. I wouldn't do it".

Before filming began on the film which had four Oscar nominations in 1977 [for Best Picture, Best Supporting Actress (Jodie Foster), Best Score (Bernard Herrmann) and Best in a Leading Role Actor (De Niro) who however, only nominations remained], after winning the Palme d'Or for best film at the Cannes Film Festival in May 1976 (in which the American playwright, president of the jury, worried about the negative influence that violent films could have on society, he commented: "The mid-1970s was characterized by some films whose violence had rarely been seen before": although he did not explicitly refer to *Taxi Driver*, it was evident that the main target of his comment was the film of Scorsese and his concerns were unfortunately met five years later with the story of the attempted assassination of Reagan).

Scorsese and De Niro set about looking for places to shoot the exteriors of the films and the actor even decided to take a license to drive the taxi in order to be more convincing as a driver.

In fact, Robert went to the Motor Vehicle Department, deposited his fingerprints as required by law and, for a few weeks, he went around New York in a taxi trying to capture from every passenger even the smallest detail that could have helped him in the role.

Nobody recognized him, which made him happy, except in a couple of circumstances.

I am generally a taciturn man, but in the taxi I chatted with my clients and learned a lot. (Robert De Niro responding to a London interviewer)

De Niro's interpretation was praised as superlative and was also appreciated for its quality of making even the twisted and violent aspects of his character acceptable.

De Niro gives the role a precise blend of embarrassment, naivety and violence that makes Travis a character who is compelling even when he's most revolting. (Variety)

Beyond the significant collaboration with Scorsese, De Niro thus recalls the relationship with another great director, Michael Cimino, who directed him in 1978 in *The Deer Hunter*: "We were willing to meet anywhere and at any time to work together".

At the end of the 1970s, "the wound of Vietnam" began to heal, the problem of television competition no longer arose and the cinema, therefore, could begin to work on this topic.

The first wave of films that dealt directly with the theme of the Vietnam War arrived in 1978-1979, with the release of the two most representative films of this period: *Apocalypse Now* and *The Deer Hunter*. These two films share some characteristics: the two directors place their works outside the tradition of the war film, refusing to tell the war through the codes of realism, characteristic of the war genre, choosing instead a symbolic representation. Furthermore, the two protagonists are not inexperienced young recruits who have to go through a training course, as happens in most war films, but they are two mature heroes, two adult fighters. (See A. RAIMONDI, R. RAIMONDI, *The Vietnam*

War Movies, Vol. 1 in «About the Vietnam War», Italy, 2021).

Cimino wanted to cast De Niro for *The Deer Hunter* and thus managed to convince him:

Michael sent me the script with a photograph of a boy with a deer tied over the hood of a White Cadillac, with some steel mills in the background. It was a great photo. (Robert De Niro)

Together they began the search for places where to shoot some exteriors, favoring the cities where steel mills were located, since some sequences of the first part of the film had to describe the life of the protagonists in the factory. In two Ohio cities, Steubenville and Mingo Junction, they studied workers' lives for six weeks and one of them was even hired to play the part of Axel in the film (Chuck Aspegren). The story takes place in 1968 in a fictional Pennsylvania town, Clairton, where the descendants of a community of Slavic immigrants live. The long scene of the wedding reception (about an hour of screening) that occupies the entire first part of the film was heavily criticized.

It is a pragmatic idea to solve the functional problem of character development. In most contemporary films there are one or two main characters, here I had at least half a dozen. To allow the audience to know them well enough, they had to be given a minimum of screen presence. The function of this hour is to let us share their life, before letting us share their nightmare. (Michael Cimino in an interview with Positif explaining the reason for this choice)

The war scenes were shot in Thailand instead because Vietnam was still considered too dangerous. De Niro and Savage did not want the help of stunt doubles for the river jump sequence despite protests from stunt coordinator Buddy Van Horn for the danger of the action and furthermore, the scene suffered a further complication due to an accident on the 'helicopter, remembered by De Niro as follows: «The skates under the helicopter got caught on the rope of a bridge which was raised and twisted while John and I were still hanging from the helicopter. It was dangerous. I looked down and yelled, "Jump!" And we jumped (…) In movies this can also happen. You have to be very, very careful. Nobody plans an accident.

You can even die with these scenes and when the audience looks at them they don't even realize how dangerous they are».

Fortunately there were many boats in the river and De Niro and Savage were suddenly rescued.

Since, as already mentioned, in 1978 the war was still an unpopular topic, Cimino had to turn to the English production company EMI which financed the project for over 7 million dollars, then winning the New York Critics' Award for best film of the year.

The Deer Hunter is the first film about Vietnam free from any political hypocrisy and capable of demolishing the moral and ideological clichés of an era. (Time Magazine)

However, there were also negative reactions, especially from some liberal periodicals, which began to label *The Deer Hunter* as a racist, a film that portrayed exclusively the Vietcong as war criminals.

The Vietcong become the murderers and torturers, and the Americans, instead, their valiant victims. (The New York Times)

The Deer Hunter is a western in which the Vietnamese Communists are the Indians, the savages who must be mow down. (Commonweal)

However, the film also managed to shake the spirits of Vietnam veterans who went to see it and aroused the indignant protest of the American Slavic community.

The scene that more than any other had sparked the most bitter controversies was that of Russian roulette, judged to be too violent and, in the opinion of the real veterans, completely improbable.

There are some who testify to having lived through those moments and others who find it inconceivable that this could have happened. For me it was a way to shock the viewer, to the point of removing the block on this war that had persisted for some time. Do not forget that for the Americans, Vietnam had fallen into a kind of anonymity due to the news footage from the front every day. (Michael Cimino)

De Niro, interpreting Michael Vronsky, offers a charismatic performance that manages to capture the attention of the viewer without making him distract even for a moment.

De Niro's acting is here perhaps his most complete. When his strength explodes against Vietnamese torturers it is terrifying. (Newsweek)

De Niro was contacted by director David Jones for his participation in the film he intended to make on the problems of reintegrating Vietnam veterans, *Jacknife* (1989). The actor had to play the character of Joseph Megessey, known by all by the nickname of "Megs", which he preferred over the other of "Jacknife" with which he was called in Vietnam, indicating a switchblade, a symbol par excellence violence repressed and ready to explode, the murderous attack and aggression. In a timeless, poor, hard-working Connecticut, Megs is a bearded mechanic with repressed energies, Dave drowns in alcohol his unquenchable despair over the loss of his best friend in Vietnam, and his sister Martha teaches in the local high school but above all she patiently acts as a cook, consoler and waitress for her brother.

Megs, also not completely recovered from the psychological after-effects of the war, tries to save his friend from his alcoholic abulia with the strength of vitality and marginally but sincerely, he woos Martha with awkwardness and tenderness, choosing for himself the philosophy of oblivion .

Megs doesn't want to remember, even if he does, sporadically hanging out with a group of former veterans and making a commitment to keep "Jacknife" under control.

The visits to Dave's house however end up giving birth to this "love story", initially hampered by Dave who considers his friend to be unsuitable for his sister.

The screenplay of the film, written by Stephen Metcalfe who originally made it into a stage work, has a major gap which is that of making the viewer understand too late the reason for Megs' interest in Dave. Only towards the end will it be known that Dave was responsible in Vietnam for the death of a mutual friend of theirs, an explanation that finally gives meaning to the development of the previous events. On the other hand, it is not clear why Megs' strong interest arose only fifteen years after their return to America.

Jacknife, which appears as the sequel to *The Deer Hunter*, therefore does not have the power and depth of Cimino's masterpiece.

When I did The Deer Hunter, I spent a lot of time with the veterans, but that was eleven years ago. They didn't talk about certain things then. Feelings come to the surface now too. So in a certain sense, this film is a continuation of the other, it tells what happens to a man who has been back home for some time. The men who still don't pay attention are the veterans. They suffer in silence. I can tell you that they don't like being taken for mad. I don't think the Vietnam War was a just war. I think it was a war we got involved in and we couldn't get out of. Many people have suffered. It was a big mistake for us to be there. (Robert De Niro, during an interview to promote Jacknife).

The solidarity that De Niro showed towards the veterans of Vietnam was particularly appreciated by them, who, on May 25, 1989, presented the actor with their Vetty Award to reward his artistic commitment.

TAXI DRIVER

The whole conviction of my life now

rests upon the belief that loneliness,

far from being a rare and curious

phenomenon, is the central and

inevitable fact of human existence.

(Thomas Wolfe, "God's Lonely Man")

In Martin Scorsese's *Taxi Driver* (1976) the Vietnamese war is not explicitly shown.

This happens in other films, but few films have represented with the same incisive crudeness, the traumas it had produced on its veterans.

The nightmares of the lived tragedy push the protagonist Travis Bickle (Robert De Niro), a taxi driver from New York, to apply his law on the streets of the Big Apple causing a carnage of thugs and thus becoming a hero in the newspapers.

The madness and violence of the protagonist, alone, alienated and misunderstood, beautifully express the thoughts and feelings of American veterans.

Scorsese's direction tells, with skepticism and raw realism, the New York at night, its dangers and its scum.

The great expressive power of the director, his ability to tell Good and Evil, but above all his letting a kind of heroism, of "distant" good, of the possibility of redemption in his characters, meander in every form of evil they are banal bad guys, but paradoxically they are "bad guys of honor".

De Niro, and his splendid portrayal of "lone wolf" in a desperate and unsuccessful attempt at human communication, Paul Schrader's script and photography make this film a masterpiece.

When Schrader conceived the idea of *Taxi Driver* he was on the verge of a nervous breakdown: his marriage had failed and the writer fell into such a depressive state that it made him sleepless and led him to wander the streets at night by car of Los Angeles, from bar to bar, before ending his nights in red light cinemas.

What saved him was an ulcer that forced him to hospital, prompted him to decide to leave Los Angeles and get back to writing. Right at that moment, Schrader completed the project of a film about his experience, which had as its protagonist the typical existential hero of European literature (thanks also to a previous re-reading of "La Nausèe", a novel by Sartre), but to be recontextualized in America, in a world completely devoid of a cultural basis capable of making him elaborate the so-called living sickness (partly inspired, among other things, by Arthur Bremer, the psychopath who in 1972 shot Alabama governor George Wallace).

His Travis Bickle is a boy tormented by an incomprehensible self-destructive impulse that he directs towards others rather than towards himself: Vietnam becomes the fundamental element to contextualize the film from a historical point of view, but the existential pessimism of the protagonist could have its origin from infinite different causes and the story of *Taxi Driver* could be set in any era.

Travis, in fact, according to Schrader, is "the man who takes anyone everywhere for money, who moves around the city like a rat in the sewer, constantly surrounded by people and yet has no friends". Like St. George on his white horse who goes across the sea to kill the dragon and save the princess of Trebizond; like Theseus who frees Ariadne by killing the Minotaur; like Aeneas carrying Anchises on her shoulders, carrying with him the ashes of his ancestors, crosses the sea and founds Rome; like Parsifal,

Lancelot, Lohengrin, following the prototype of the unblemished and fearless knight, with honor and moral strength, but above all with the imperishable desire to always make the good triumph, even Travis in *Taxi Driver* can be defined as a knight. However, he is a modern knight from the seventies.

He is not a hero, he is an anti-hero. He is a romantic hero, so to speak, an individual outside his society and conventions. In the 70s, people showed a great interest in the anti-hero, in a character they identified with and could feel the pain of him, whose suffering was not unique but of all. Travis Bickle's pain comes from his loneliness, his alienation, his being different, his inability to integrate and give meaning to his life. Like Raskol'nikov (protagonist of the novel "Crime and Punishment" by Fyodor Dostoevsky), in a parallelism between the St. Petersburg of the defenseless, the humble, the poor people, wooden houses, unhealthy environments in the nineteenth century and New York over the years Seventies, Travis has a peculiar psychological condition.

PERSONNEL OFFICER: So what do you wanna hack for, Bickle?

TRAVIS: I can't sleep nights.

PERSONNEL OFFICER: There's porno theaters for that.

TRAVIS: I know. I tried that.

PERSONNEL OFFICER: So what do you do now?

TRAVIS: Now? Ride around nights mostly. Subways, buses. Figure I might as well get paid for it.

PERSONNEL OFFICER: You wanna work uptown? South Bronx, Harlem?

TRAVIS: I'll work anytime, anywhere.

PERSONNEL OFFICER: Will you work Jewish holidays?

TRAVIS: Anytime, anywhere.

PERSONNEL OFFICER: Let me see your chauffeur's license. How's your record?

TRAVIS: It's clean. It's real clean, like my conscience. (*Taxi Driver*, 1976)

Travis is a maladjusted boy, a Vietnam veteran suffering from post-traumatic stress disorder, the so-called war neurosis, with symptoms ranging from insomnia, depression and numbness, but is also plagued by schizoid personality disorder, characterized by a form of acute distress, bizarre behavior and inability to form close relationships with others, by a constant brooding over one's thoughts.

TRAVIS: Loneliness has followed me my whole life. Everywhere. In bars, in cars, sidewalks, stores, everywhere. There's no escape. I'm God's lonely man. (*Taxi Driver*, 1976)

His is a self-inflicted loneliness, a behavioral syndrome that reinforces itself and the typical elements of this attitude can be traced back to a series of contradictory impulses: puritanism and pornography at the same time, getting back into shape and stuffing oneself with pills, such as tranquilizers and psychotropic drugs (as if he wanted to strengthen his condition as a convict).

After all, the retaliation of the hero's nobility and audacity is solitude: the necessary solitude that alienates the protagonist from the contemporary world, from the contemporary.

Here is his heroism: his alienation, his being maladjusted from the context in which he lives that allow him to face it.

Travis, however, is exasperated by this loneliness: he can not find any possibility to speak, to communicate, to dialogue with others.

```
TRAVIS: All my life needed was a
sense of someplace to go. I don't
believe that one should devote his
life to morbid self-attention. I
believe that someone should become a
person like other people. (Taxi Driver,
1976)
```

Only in a crowded environment can there be real loneliness.

Only by being together with so many people does one feel truly alone.

In chaotic New York, Travis is surrounded by a lot of passersby, but he feels alone.

TRAVIS: Twelve hours of work and I still can't sleep. Damn. Days go on and on. They don't end. (*Taxi Driver*, 1976)

Travis suffers from insomnia and therefore decides to spend the night hours working as a taxi driver in New York.

TRAVIS: Each night when I return the cab to the garage, I have to clean the cum off the back seat. Some nights, I clean off the blood. (*Taxi Driver*, 1976)

However, he is an attentive taxi driver who observes and analyzes the world.

He is an intelligent person, with refined thinking, perhaps also thanks to his habit of having a personal diary in which he transcribes his thoughts, but he comes, unfortunately, from a difficult reality, that of the Vietnam War.

He is neither an Italian American nor a Catholic, he is just a lonely man who is not part of any ethnic or religious community, of any group.

He is a very complex, disturbing, racist, introverted but sympathetic character who, between moments of vulnerability, self-pity, anger and disgust, despite the traumas due to the horrors of war, in his obsessions and desperation, exploring every corner and side of humanity that populates New York tries to reflect, in the night, at the worst moment, in the darkest one, in which all the vices, defects and disgust of the city re-emerge.

TRAVIS: May 10th. Thank God for the rain which has helped wash away the garbage and trash off the sidewalks. I'm workin' long hours now, six in the afternoon to six in the morning. Sometimes even eight in the morning, six days a week. Sometimes seven days a week. It's a long hustle but it keeps me real busy. I can take in three, three fifty a week. Sometimes even more when I do it off the meter. All the animals come out at night - whores, skunk pussies, buggers, queens, fairies, dopers, junkies, sick, venal. Someday a real rain will come and wash all this scum off the streets. I go all over.

I take people to the Bronx, Brooklyn, I take 'em to Harlem. I don't care. Don't make no difference to me. It does to some. Some won't even take spooks. Don't make no difference to me. (*Taxi Driver*, 1976)

The city represents all that is forbidden and crazy and Travis, tired of the wickedness he sees in the world, cannot accept its filth, its filthy reality, which needs to be cleaned of moral decay, by now without any inhibitory restraint.

New York portrays that internal crisis of the city that is strictly connected to that more general decline of the whole nation.

The New York of the seventies was plagued by a multiplicity of social and economic problems, from extreme inflation to high unemployment, to exaggerated crime and violence, constantly on the rise. In the protagonist, all this hatred, this rancor, this anger, this racism come from the war, in which there is this aversion towards the enemy, this desire to destroy the hated object, but also this desire to escape from the "different".

This is why, sometimes, those who hate and in this case, the one who was taught to hate, Travis, this twenty-six year old Vietnam veteran, feels entitled to break the law to punish the objects of his hatred, as he feels, in the his social inadequacy, in his detachment from reality, being himself an outcast, of not doing something wrong, of acting "according to justice", lashing out at those "different" individuals on whom society discharges the blame for all evils. In this "urban" film, the camera lingers on constantly humid outdoor environments, in which the water smears instead of washing, making streets and men even more slippery. Urban places appear seedy and decadent (the streets, bars, snack bars, third-rate cinemas and underground parking lots) and the natural world is almost non-existent, as crumbling and claustrophobic interiors are privileged (such as the apartment of Travis and the room where Iris works), with artificial, violent and saturated colors to highlight the fact that the city precludes the escape or inhibits the mobility of the characters, both from a spiritual and physical/geographical point of view. Moreover, for example, when Travis talks on the phone, the camera moves and frames an empty corridor, or we consider the scenes in slow motion: everything, in short, contributes to making a documentary of the protagonist's mind. Much like a western hero, Travis quickly identifies his community's problems and his cab rides match those cowboy rides through thug-studded towns. Not only are the streets full of hostile individuals and prostitutes, but even the cinema signs constantly allude to violence, blood and pornography. The protagonist, although he travels all the time, does not get anywhere, as his taxi turns to streets towards which he feels nothing, only a strong sense of disgust.

With no real social relationship, except for chatting with colleagues between races, with this loneliness that haunts him and to which he believes he is inexorably destined, in his existential pessimism, Travis still feels a feeble but ardent desire to love (wonderfully indicated by Bernard Herrmann's romantic soundtrack) that pushes him to seek, in the human totality, disgusting and corrupt that moves as in a horrifying nocturnal parade before his eyes, an authentic and genuine human contact, able to tear apart his empty existence made up of work, insomnia and moments of leisure in the red light cinemas.

```
 TRAVIS:    I    first    saw    her    at
Palantine   Campaign   headquarters   at
63rd and Broadway. She was wearing a
white   dress.   She   appeared   like   an
angel. Out of this filthy mess, she
is alone. They... cannot... touch...
her. (Taxi Driver, 1976)
```

In this New York, apparently sparkling, but actually characterized by superficiality, indifference and distrust, there is therefore only one girl with whom Travis manages to communicate: the charming Betsy (Cybill Shepherd), who is part of the electoral staff of Senator Charles Palantine.

In Betsy, Travis sees a lifeline, a glimmer of light to cling to to reach a paradise, a feeling of peace that saves him, that makes him flee from the metropolitan chaos of a seedy New York, whose lights, at night, they symbolically illuminate the streets and sidewalks with reddish and bluish tones, making it hell, the earthly embodiment of Evil.

Red is the predominant color of the film, as it symbolizes the brutal conflict between love and hate that fuels the hero's deeds. The girl also works in the election campaign for Palantine and therefore Travis begins to see also in the political, a positive change, a bulwark of salvation, just like Betsy who advertises it.

However, Betsy belongs to a different social class: awkward, with numerous difficulties, Travis, pretending to be a supporter of Palantine, manages to win a date, but wrecked miserably because of his loneliness and his "plebeian" tastes, not realizing the diversity of girl. He cannot break away from his daily monotony, to momentarily leave out his clumsy behavioral patterns and then naively leads Betsy even to watch a dirty movie, thinking that what he likes must necessarily like her too. Travis does not identify with Betsy who is scandalized, he is too stuck in his mental schemes and their meeting turns out to be a failure, a disappointment, also due to the coldness of the girl.

TRAVIS: I realize now how much she's just like the others. Cold and

distant, and many people are like
that. Women for sure. They're like a
union. (*Taxi Driver*, 1976)

Betsy's refusal, who no longer answers his
phone calls, makes her pathological dimension
even more pervasive.

TRAVIS: I tried several times to
call her, but after the first call,
she wouldn't come to the phone any
longer. I also sent flowers but with
no luck. The smell of the flowers
only made me sicker. The headaches
got worse. I think I got stomach
cancer. I shouldn't complain though.
You're only as healthy, you're only
as healthy as you feel. You're only
as... healthy... as... you... feel.
(*Taxi Driver*, 1976)

After meeting a passenger who has murderous
instincts towards his wife who betrays him
(played by Scorsese himself; as George Memmoli
was originally supposed to play the character,
but he fell and got hurt), in Travis' mind it clicks
like a mechanism that he tries to communicate

outside to a colleague during the night. Here is his mental confusion and his growing isolation, the externalization of the ethical-moral dilemmas and conflicts of the Vietnam veteran, abandoned by the institutions and unable to reconnect social relations: Travis tries to express his discomfort to his older colleague Wizard (Peter Boyle) who, however, fails to advise him usefully.

TRAVIS: (...) I got some bad ideas in my head (...) (*Taxi Driver*, 1976)

Travis, a "lucid" patient in a sick society, in his monologues, in his flow of thoughts, begins to develop a desire for revenge towards that wrong reality. Travis is the man who, unable to lead a joyful and carefree life, spontaneously chooses to make an existential sacrifice to take revenge for the external projection of that same evil from which he cannot free himself.

TRAVIS: June 8th. My life has taken another turn again. The days move along with regularity, over and over, one day indistinguishable from the next. A long, continuous chain. And then suddenly there is change.

```
TRAVIS: June 29th. I gotta get in
shape now. Too much sittin' is
ruinin' my body. Too much abuse has
gone on for too long. From now on,
it will be fifty push-ups each
morning, fifty pull-ups. There'll be
no more pills, there'll be no more
bad food, no more destroyers of my
body. From now on, it will be total
organization. Every muscle must be
tight.
```
 (*Taxi Driver*, 1976)

The primary target of Travis' wrath, from the point of view of the disappointed and angry veteran, becomes Senator Palantine, the emblem of that demagogy, of that hypocritical politics at the basis of the squalor and decay of the society in which he is forced to live.

```
TRAVIS: The idea had been growing
in my brain for some time. True
force. All the king's men cannot put
it back together again.
```
 (*Taxi Driver*, 1976)

A past event particularly disturbs the restless mind of the taxi driver: a very young prostitute named Iris who had tried to escape from her patron, a certain Matthew "Sport" (Harvey

Keitel), getting into Travis' taxi and nevertheless being led violently out of the criminal, who left him ten dollars on the seat to make him "forget" what he had seen. Iris was played by the already talented Jodie Foster, persecuted repeatedly in real life, after the shooting of the film, by her peculiar admirer, John Hinckley, who in 1981, immediately after Reagan's attack, explained at the time of the arrest of having seen *Taxi Driver* fifteen times, having developed the idea of murder and therefore having wanted to emulate Bickle to get noticed by the actress. Iris, this twelve-and-a-half-year-old girl, ran away from her family and found refuge in New York, where she is forced to prostitute herself with the trick of the slimy Sport, which made her believe that he was in love with her and her plunged into the spiral of drug addiction. The continuous vision of this young prostitute on the streets of New York becomes an obsession, but also one of the decisive moments that will slowly bring out the latent heroism of Travis, who will conceive a murder/suicide against the senator: still prostrate due to disappointment received from Betsy, he will begin to see in Palantine and in his speeches the symbol of the ethical and moral crisis of the contemporary world, false and illusory. Travis would like to kill him, then being killed, in turn, by the escort service, thus leaving all his money as an inheritance to Iris to allow her to escape and rebuild a life.

TRAVIS: (Travis is trying his guns on the mirror) Huh? Huh? (Draws) Faster than you, fucking son of a... Saw you coming you fucking... shitheel. (Reholsters) I'm standing here; you make the move. You make the move. It's your move... (Draws) Don't try it you fuck. (Reholsters) You talkin' to me? You talkin' to me? You talkin' to me? Then who the hell else are you talking... you talking to me? Well I'm the only one here. Who the fuck do you think you're talking to? Oh yeah? OK. (Draws). (*Taxi Driver*, 1976)

Travis seems to threaten and threaten himself in front of the mirror, a disturbing and privileged element that offers the opportunity to duplicate places and people with a confused and ambiguous perceptual purpose. Without the protagonist's threatening reflection, it seems that he, looking at the camera, is addressing directly to the passive and indifferent viewer that he does not have the courage to rebel.

Or, in front of the mirror, with all possible and imaginable weapons, through this peculiar spiritual dimension, with this mirroring and turning to himself, Travis is actually addressing the world and asking him to communicate with him, to speak, almost in a sort of prayer, of invocation, in the concrete affirmation of his existence, of which someone, perhaps, now, has finally realized.

TRAVIS: Listen, you fuckers, you screwheads. Here is a man who would not take it anymore. A man who stood up against the scum, the cunts, the dogs, the filth, the shit. Here is a man who stood up. (*Taxi Driver*, 1976)

In Travis, the desire to clean up the world and change things is getting stronger and finally his moment seems to have arrived, the opportunity he had been waiting for so long.

Just like Saint George saving the princess from the dragon, in a sort of deterioration of the protagonists of the story (a traumatized and disturbed Vietnam veteran who wants to save a young prostitute, in a context that is also degraded and degrading), like that knight without stain and fearless, Travis finds a young girl who, although a very young prostitute, has the naivety, candor, amazement, naivety and even stupidity of any girl of that age and he is willing to do anything what to save her. On a rainy evening, Travis, by chance in a supermarket of an acquaintance, with the newly bought gun, during a robbery, kills a black criminal and the merchant invites him to leave the crime scene and then he takes it out on the lifeless body of the thief, cursing and hitting him with an iron stick, in a "normal" violence and racism, horribly shared and approved.

Walt Whitman, that great American poet spoke for all of us when he said "I am the man. I suffered. I was there." Today I say to you: we are the people. We suffered. We were there. We, the people, suffered in Vietnam. We, the people, suffered. We still suffer from unemployment, inflation, crime and corruption.

TRAVIS: Dear Father and Mother: July is the month I remember which brings not only your wedding anniversary but also Father's Day and Mother's birthday. I'm sorry I can't remember the exact dates, but I hope this card will take care of them all. I'm sorry again I cannot send you my address like I promised to last year. But the sensitive nature of my work for the government demands utmost secrecy. I know you will understand. I am healthy and well and making lots of money. I have been going with a girl for several months and I know you would be proud if you could see her. Her name is Betsy but I can tell you no more than that... I hope this card finds you all well as it does me. I hope no one has died. Don't worry about me. One day, they'll be a knock on the door and it'll be me. Love Travis. (*Taxi Driver*, 1976)

In the moment in which Travis chooses to reorganize his life, his first victim is his own television, a symbol of a false society and destroying it, he also eliminates a world without values that darkens the minds and no longer distinguishes the true from the false. Travis then decides to meet the pimp (Keitel specially grew the nail of his little finger, used to put up cocaine and dressed just like a pimp he had often observed in the past) and therefore Iris to convince her to change her life.

TRAVIS: Your name Matthew? I want some action.

SPORT: Officer, I swear I'm clean. I'm just waiting here for a friend. You're gonna bust me for nothing, man?

TRAVIS: I'm not a cop. I aint't a…

SPORT: Then why are you asking me for action?

TRAVIS:… Because she sent me over (pointing to Iris).

SPORT: I suppose that ain't a .38 you got in your sock.

TRAVIS: .38? I'm clean, man.

SPORT: Shit, you're a real cowboy? That's nice, man. All right. That's all right. 15 dollars, 15 minutes. 25 dollars, half an hour.

TRAVIS: Shit.

SPORT: Cowboy, huh? I once had a horse, on Coney Island. She got hit by a car. Well, take it or leave it. If you wanna save yourself some money, don't fuck her.

(...)

TRAVIS: I'm hip.

SPORT: (laughing) Funny, you don't look hip.

(Travis stands still) Have yourself a good time. Go ahead, man.

You're a funny guy. But looks aren't everything. Go ahead, man. Have a good time. (*Taxi Driver*, 1976)

Travis, of course, instead of having sex with Iris, tries to persuade her to change her life, but she doesn't want to be helped, explaining that maybe she was on drugs when she tried to escape and that Sport, her protector/lover, takes great care her.

(…)

TRAVIS: Listen I… Can't you understand something? You came into my cab. You wanted to get out of here.

IRIS: I must've been stoned.

TRAVIS: Why? They drug you?

(…)

TRAVIS: Damn it! Don't you want out of here? Can you understand why I'm here?

IRIS: I think I understand. I tried to get into your cab and now you wanna come and take me away. Is that it?

(…)

TRAVIS: Well look, can I see you again?

IRIS: That's not hard to do.

TRAVIS: Not like that. I mean, you know, regularly. This is nothing for a person to do.

IRIS: How about breakfast tomorrow?

TRAVIS: Tomorrow?

IRIS: I get up at 1:00.

TRAVIS: One o'clock? Well, I got that thing. I don't know (…) One o'clock. Okay. See you tomorrow. Oh, Iris. My name is Travis.

IRIS: Thanks a lot, Travis.

TRAVIS: So long, Iris. See you tomorrow. Sweet Iris. (*Taxi Driver*, 1976)

The next morning, Travis and Iris meet as agreed. The way of speaking, the girl's sunglasses, the bread with sugar and jam, the fact that she was drugged, was all inspired by a real blonde and very thin prostitute, thanks to which, her theoretician character actually became real.

IRIS: Why do you want me to go back to my parents? They hate me. Why do you think I split? There ain't nothing there.

TRAVIS: But you can't live like this. It's a hell. A girl should live at home.

IRIS: Didn't you ever hear of women's lib?

TRAVIS: What do you mean, "women's lib"? You're a young girl. You should be at home now. You should be dressed up, going out with boys. You should be going to school. You know, that kind of stuff.

IRIS: Oh, God, are you square.

TRAVIS: I'm not square. You're square. You're full of shit, man. What do you mean? You walk out with fucking creeps, lowlifes and degenerates and you sell your little pussy for nothing, man? For some low-life pimp? Stands in a hall. I'm square? You're the one that's square, man. I don'to go screw and fuck with killers and junkies like you. You call that being hip? What world you from?

(...)

IRIS: Sport never treated me bad. He didn't beat me up once.

TRAVIS: But you can't allow him to do the same to other girls. You can't allow him to do that. He's the lowest kind of person. Somebody's got to do something to him. He's the scum of the earth. He's the worst… sucking scum I have ever, ever seen. You know what he told me about you? He called you names. He called you a little piece of chicken.

(…)

TRAVIS: I'll give you the money to go.

IRIS: You don't have to.

TRAVIS: I want you to take it. I don't want you to take anything from them and I wanna do it. I don't have anything better to do with my money. I might be going away for a while. (*Taxi Driver*, 1976)

Travis burns the roses that were once a gift for Betsy inside his home. They, symbol of Love, Passion and Paradise, but also, according to popular medieval superstition and many folkloristic legends, were the favorite flowers of witches, suitable for causing Evil and Hate thanks to the presence on their stem of many thorns and burning, become the representation of the deepest and most intimate contradictions at the basis of the attribution of a moral relevance (positive and negative) to human deeds, conditioned by circumstances, which end up determining the value of a man more than his real intentions.

Travis then writes this letter to Iris:

Dear Iris, this money should be enough for your trip. By the time you read this I will be dead. Travis

To assassinate Palantine, to fulfill his mission, Travis, meanwhile, got the iconic Mohawk haircut, just like those guys who went to Vietnam, in the jungle, to perform certain missions and cut their hair like that and easily recognizable, they looked like Mohicans.

TRAVIS: Now I see it clearly. My whole life is pointed in one direction. I see that now. There never has been ant choice for me.
(*Taxi Driver*, 1976)

The attack, however, was immediately thwarted as Travis was immediately spotted by the armed guards in the crowd, despite the fact that he still managed to escape.

The story ends in a great violence: Travis makes his suicidal fantasies come true as a psychopath. Paradoxically, as the moment of the massacre approaches, the protagonist becomes almost mute and no longer seems to be writing his diary, as if in his vehemence he could no longer maintain verbal control of the events. Before, however, his diary and his narrating voice "in the present" told us his story just as it took place, also overlapping the images of New York, appearing as the only honest character in the film, judge of people and events (seen almost exclusively through his eyes and his vision of reality) and thus also altering the emotional perception of the spectator, who gradually accessed Travis' mind and his distorted vision of a homicidal mission.

His "redeeming complex", his feeling called to carry out a salvific, almost Christological mission, his heroism/anti-heroism is now concretized in his apotheosis, in his moment of glory, in a world of triumphal bloodshed, including his own, in an ending of pathological and suicidal glory, beyond realism and social values, beyond what is right and what is wrong, beyond Good and Evil. Back home, after the failed attack, Travis decides to change plans: the same evening, he goes to the area, in the building where Iris works, provokes his pimp and shoots him a shot in the abdomen.

TRAVIS: Hey, Sport, how you doing?

SPORT: Okay, okay, my man. How… Where do I know you from, man?

TRAVIS: I don't know. How's everything in the pimp business?

SPORT: Do I know you?

TRAVIS: No. Do I know you?

SPORT: Get out of here. Get lost.

TRAVIS: Do I know you? How's Iris? You know Iris.

SPORT: No, I don't know nobody named Iris. Iris? Come on, get out of here, man.

TRAVIS: You don't know Iris?

SPORT: I don't know nobody named Iris.

TRAVIS: No?

SPORT: Get back to your tribe before you get hurt. I don't want no trouble, okay?

TRAVIS: You got a gun?

SPORT: (Sport throws the cigarette he was smoking against his jacket and kicks him) Get the fuck out of here, man! Get out of here!

TRAVIS: Suck on this. (Travis shoots him) . (*Taxi Driver*, 1976)

So, after stopping for a few moments on the stairs of the building, Travis goes up to the girl's room and, now out of his mind, also shoots the guest house, wounding him. However, he is, in turn, smeared in the neck by Sport, who in the meantime has arrived behind him, bleeding but still alive, being immediately killed by Travis.

Then, he slaughters a mobster who was in the room with Iris, after the latter had wounded him in his arm.

Finally, arrived in Iris' room, Travis finishes the guest house, who had miserably followed him, first stabbing his hand with the knife and then firing a shot in the head, despite the Iris' desperate pleading not to do so. After the mission, Travis attempts to commit suicide, but all the guns at his disposal have run out of ammunition and seriously but not fatally wounded, he lies exhausted on the sofa, where he watches the police officers rushed for the shooting.

In the silent sequence following the massacre, accompanied only by Herrmann's music, the carnage just carried out by Travis (inspired by the final scenes of Peckinpah's 1969 *The Wild*

Bunch) is retraced backwards, with blood on the walls, weapons on the ground and corpses.

The protagonist is no longer on stage and this fading, strongly in contrast with the previous monocular vision of reality, refers to the fact that in the clash with the world, the anti-hero, finally putting into practice his ideals of revenge and purification, disappears after completing his mission.

Dear Mr. Bickle,

I can't say how happy Mrs. Steensma and I were to hear that you are well and recuperating. We tried to visit you at the hospital when we were in New York to pick up Iris but you were still in a coma. There is no way we can repay you for returning our Iris to us. We thought we had lost her and now our lives are full again. Needless to say you are something of a hero around this household. I'm sure you want to know about Iris. She's back in school and working hard. The transition has been very hard for her as you can well imagine. But we have taken steps to see she has never cause to run away again. In conclusion, Mrs. Steensma and I would like to again thank you from the bottom of our hearts. Unfortunately, we cannot afford to come to New York again to thank you in person, or we surely would. But if you should ever come to Pittsburgh you would find yourself a most welcome guest in our home.

Our deepest thanks,

Burt and Ivy Steensma

(Letter from Iris' father to Travis. *Taxi Driver*, 1976)

Travis' mission has been divulged and deformed by the media ("TAXI DRIVER BATTLES GANGSTERS/REPUTED NEW YORK MAFIOSO KILLED IN BIZARRE SHOOTING/TAXI DRIVER HERO TO RECOVER"): through a kind of massacre, in an incredible paradox, from a dangerous character, from a neurotic misfit, he has become a citizen hero, because in the world of media, fame and celebrity, there are values. Travis Bickle, in fact, despite being a psychopath and trying to kill the senator and killing simple passersby in a brothel, has become a hero because he is famous.

In the last sequence of the film, with an intertwining of voices and glances between man and woman, there is the meeting between Betsy and Travis in the taxi.

The protagonist does not tell the story of her to the girl, he communicates with her only through the rearview mirror, as if she had once again become a lilial figure for him.

Betsy, who had rejected him when he was not yet famous, now admires him, looks for him, but the anti-hero, precisely for this absurd society that instead of recognizing his illness, has proclaimed him a hero, even allows himself to abandon, like all true heroes, even the girl of his ideals and to leave in the night with his taxi, silent and inscrutable. However, in the last shot there is a sudden shot of Travis, with a very close-up of his disturbing eyes reflected in the rearview mirror: he has not changed. He is not healed. After his shocking gaze and the reflections of the nocturnal "hell city", the credits appear with the double image of New York now flowing in front of the windshield as if imprisoned in the reflection of the mirror.

Once his task is finished, Travis seems neither stronger nor satisfied or happy, indeed he even seems to have returned to the starting point, to his alienating and solitary existence.

In the failure of his decisive and apocalyptic action, life returns as before, things have not changed, as in the ghostly existence of the eternal return.

Although Travis' last troubled glance in the mirror reveals the threatening future possibility of a new outbreak of violence, even if swallowed up by the images of the night city, the "regeneration through violence" fails miserably because it is not suitable for contemporary society.

Eventually (Travis) gets screwed, as the gun is unloaded. But, over time, the cycle will start again, and next time it will succeed. The redemption or elevation he seeks is that of a teenager (…) he is not smart enough to attach meaning to it. (Paul Schrader)

Travis leaves in the taxi, sinking into the immense multicolored city. In the hope that no one will sink into the city, with a deep sense of integrity, morality, honesty, righteousness and with this desire for cleanliness, walking the ways of the world, both the darkest and the brightest, always pursue what is right, living virtuously.

THE DEER HUNTER

«ONE SHOT»

You have to think about one shot. One shot is what it's all about. A deer's gotta be taken with one shot.

The Deer Hunter by Michael Cimino (1978) can be considered one of the first Vietnam movies of the "homecoming" genre, which will characterize much of the 1980s production.

Winner of 5 Oscars for Best Film, Best Director, Best Supporting Actor (Christopher Walken), Best Sound, Best Editing and Golden Globe to Michael Cimino for Best Director, Nastro d'Argento for Best Foreign Film.

The Deer Hunter is above all the film that had the advantage of knowing how to insinuate itself into the American collective unconscious better than any other film about Vietnam, thanks to the shocking way in which the horror of war was expressed.

It is the story of six Russian friends from the small town community of Clairton, Pennsylvania (Michael/Mike, Nick, Steven,

Stanley, Axel and John) who spend a peaceful existence between working as a steel mill and hunting for deer.

The first three, Mike, Nick and Steven (respectively played by Robert De Niro, Christopher Walken and John Savage), are about to leave for Vietnam.

Steven, the most shy and awkward, is about to marry his beloved Angela, who is secretly pregnant with someone else.

Instead, Mike and Nick (the two best friends) love the same woman, Linda (Meryl Streep), who for the violence perpetrated by her abusive and alcoholic father, will move into their home following their departure.

Nick is friendly, but attentive, sensitive and profound, and yet willing to take risks, he is one who likes to bet and gamble. Instead, Mike is the respected and sometimes misunderstood leader of the group and practices the hunt with the respect and seriousness of an ancient hero: he adopts the logic of the "one shot".

NICK: For Christ's sake, Mike. Steven is getting married in a couple of hours, I don't know what the hell we're doing talking about hunting a last time before the Army. The whole thing, it's crazy.

MIKE: I'll tell you one thing. If I found out my life had to end up in the mountains, it'd be all right. But it has to be in your mind.

NICK: What? One shot?

MIKE: Two is pussy.

NICK: I don't think about one shot that much any more, Mike.

MIKE: You have to think about one shot. One shot is what it's all about. A deer's gotta be taken with one shot. I try to tell people that, they don't listen. You really think about Vietnam?

NICK: Yeah. I don't know. I guess I'm thinking about the deer. Going to Nam. I like the trees, you know? I like the way the trees are in the

```
mountains,  it's  all  different.  The
way  the  trees  are  (...)  (The Deer Hunter, 1978)
```

The other companions, with the exception of Nick, the only one with whom Mike takes pleasure in going hunting, devote themselves to it with vulgarity and slovenliness.

```
MIKE:  I'll  tell  you,  Nick,  you're
the  only  guy  I  go  hunting  with,  you
know?  I  like  a  guy  with  quick  moves
and  speed.  I  ain't  gonna  hunt  with
no  assholes.  (The Deer Hunter, 1978)
```

In the first part of the film, which develops the theme of friendship and solidarity between these men, there is a wedding party and a deer hunt, for which, according to Umberto Eco, a reference model of the film could be Война и миръ, Tolstoy's great realist novel, precisely because of that narrative and dramaturgical scansion that dedicates a good half of the film to the "noisy" peace of the wedding banquet, with dances, alcohol and friendly fights, but also for the references to the hunting trip in the Rostov estate that anticipates the Napoleonic invasion and for the emblematic setting in Pittsburgh, among workers and families of Russian origin, whose wedding ceremony is in fact Orthodox.

In church we see the faces of people we have already met and among them, our attention falls on John Welsh, the owner of the bar (where friends gather to drink beer, sing and play) who sings in the choir with his characteristic baby face and his cherub red cheeks.

During the wedding celebrations, however, we observe people singing and dancing, flirting and competing with each other, moving from one group to another, offering us memories that give us a sense of normality and familiarity, in a nostalgic and romantic vision of marriage and of life. Clairton is also a stranger to those issues that people argue about in beer bars; no one ever asks what the Americans are doing in Vietnam, there are no racial jokes and strikes, or anything else that might show dissent, anger or limitation. A small negative omen, however, manifests itself during the cheerful and wild celebrations: Steven and his bride, who is pregnant but not of him, receive wine in a double-cup chalice, from the priest, who tells them that they drink it without pouring one drop will have lifelong luck, and we see the unfortunate pouring of wine through the little stains that form on the bride's white lace bodice.

In the first part of the film, in the festive atmosphere, the theme of war is already introduced, which begins to mark the separation within the group of friends, with the three, Mike, Nick and Steven, who will leave for Vietnam.

This distancing will become more and more until it becomes unbridgeable.

Thus, the specter of war manifests itself already during the wedding party with the appearance of a green beret, a Vietnam veteran, sitting at the bar, which constitutes a disturbing element, in clear contrast with that serene and joyful context. After Steven and Angela's never-ending wedding party (where Nick asks Linda to marry him and she accepts), when Angela and Steven drive off, Nick asks Mike to make him a promise.

NICK: (…) If anithing happens, Mike, don't leave, don't leave me over

there (...) You gotta promise me that, Mike.

 MIKE: Hey, Nicky... You got it, pal.
(*The Deer Hunter*, 1978)

In the farewell scene, the five hunters return to John Welsh's bar playing a Chopin nocturne while the others listen intently: Mike, Nick, Axel, Stan (weak and insecure hitting women and killing deer) and Steven (simple and naive) demonstrate their innate sensitivity, showing us that behind the appearance of savage beer drinkers, there are feelings that they cannot express in words, but that come out here thanks to the music. It is a moment of communion before their paths part, before Vietnam.

But, before the farewell scene, very touching and emotional, in which already begins to feel this heaviness, this tragic and distressing atmosphere of the war that hangs over them and the splendid Chopin's music stops to make room for the noise of Vietnam's helicopters, friends go hunting. Stanley has forgotten his boots at home and asks Mike to borrow them, but Mike feels disgust at his companion's inattention (who will not go to Vietnam by chance), as a sign of his superficiality and extraneousness to the ethics of warriors, shared by him and Nick, the friend he is most fond of. The detachment within the group takes on a spiritual dimension, becoming existential: Mike seems to have already internalized the war and its moral principles, and like a soldier, after jokes and discussions, he kills a deer, killing it with "one blow", like he is used to hunting, that is to say with a single bullet in order to give the prey the possibility, in the case of a wrong shot, to escape and survive. A single shot is the emblem of a manly world, but only in peacetime and on hunting trips, until the protagonist Mike even gives the deer a chance, firing only one shot, and since the animal cannot defend itself, if he fails to hit it, it would be deemed safe by now. In this conception, man cannot show all his strength (among other things, not natural, as it is given to him by the weapon), he cannot bend nature, he cannot overwhelm it.

However, this logic of the single blow, from a symbol of virile loyalty, then becomes an emblem of madness in another reality, that of war, in the transition from hunting animals to hunting men, to that of the enemy, in the total loss of innocence of America with the Vietnamese conflict, so this is the terrible moment in the life of three boys from an American province who find themselves catapulted into a different world, in the Vietnam War. In Vietnam, after military action, Mike, Nick and Steven are captured by the Vietcong and forced to participate in the torture of Russian roulette, while the jailers bet on them.

Only one shot, a single pistol shot with the drum, inside which there is only a bullet that turns and when you press the trigger the head can blow up or the psyche certainly jumps. Russian roulette is in fact a very dangerous game of chance which consists in placing a single bullet in a revolver, rotating the drum quickly, closing the weapon without looking, pointing it towards one's head and then pressing the trigger. The adjective "Russian" perhaps alludes to the fact that the first description of such a practice is narrated by the great Russian poet and writer Mikhail Jur'evič Lermontov in the short story *The fatalist* in the collection, from the 1840 novel "Герой нашего времени (Geroy nashevo vremeni)" [*A Hero of Our Time*].

Lermontov tells the story of a lieutenant of the tsar's dragons, a certain Vulič, an officer of Serbian origin in the tsarist army, who, to demonstrate his faith in the immutability of destiny, holds a pistol taken from the dormitory and points it at his own head, then throwing a playing card in the air and as soon as it touches the ground, he takes the gun, spins the drum and finally pulls the trigger. Fortunately, nothing happens to the protagonist of the story: the blow fails.

These challenges of courage that seemed to transcend even duels at the time, at a time when these were still common, so much so that Lermontov himself died on July 27 of the year following the writing of his story (1841), precisely in a duel with a former partner, due to a sudden quarrel. The term "Russian roulette", however, was used for the first time in 1937 in a narration of the same name by the American author George Surdez (published in *Collier's Magazine*), in which these dangerous games of the soldiers of the French Foreign Legion were told in a constant attempt to combat boredom and tedium during their long stay in North Africa. The director of *The Deer Hunter*, Michael Cimino, seems to have a somewhat particular, curiously suggestive relationship with pistols, as demonstrated by his first two films, *Magnum Force* in 1973 (as a screenwriter) and *Thunderbolt and Lightfoot* in 1974 (at his first directing).

The innocent and almost banal life of these three friends, spoiled so to speak, who work in a steel mill with these fumes, in this Russian environment, in a remote province of Pennsylvania, hunting, drinking and getting drunk (in a sort of parallelism with the existence of a nineteenth-century Soviet nobleman, such as Lermontov, between parties and drinking) is totally upset. At the same time, the Russian roulette of Vietnam had become the game of the legionaries of the foreign region in the tedious hours, in the tormenting heat of the desert, within these remote garrisons, in which French soldiers played this game. And it is they at the end of the 1880s, when France conquered Vietnam and then the Legion landed in Tonkin and Indochina, to bring this game which then came, in a sort of mockery against the new invaders (the Americans), practiced by the Vietcong (who expelled the Foreign Legion and the French in 1954, thus obtaining independence and starting to expand southwards).

The American boys catapulted into Vietnam were not used to the dirty war, the war in the jungle, a gang conflict led by a devastated people who fight as best they can, using every weapon and every brutality, with the power and ferocity of the mold Eastern, in a clash between different cultures (on the one hand, the Western one, of well-being and on the other the Eastern one, the Vietnamese one, with immense endurance and resistance to atrocities, effort, fatigue, sacrifice, pain and to despair). So, these three friends lost in this paradoxical context, in this ferocious and bloody carnival, in which, when they are taken prisoner, they are reified, mocked, slapped, vilified and forced by the Vietcong to play that imported game of death right by westerners. Vietnamese soldiers are often shown with poor visibility so that it is very difficult to distinguish them, they are all the same and dehumanized, and their words, their cries appear incomprehensible.

In this physical and psychological trap, Steven is the first to give in, when, overwhelmed by terror and exhaustion, he fires at the ceiling the blow he should have brought to the head according to the rules of the merciless game and so, as a punishment, he is thrown in a cage immersed in the river and full of mice. Mike, on the other hand, with coldness and lucidity, in order to be able to obtain his freedom and that of his friends, planning things in advance and not caring about the risks, persuades Nick to try to escape, by inserting three bullets in the drum in order to kill their captors, however increasing the risk of being killed during the game.

The desperate plan is successful and after freeing Steven, the three, attached to a tree trunk, run away letting themselves be carried away by the current of the river. Arriving at a suspension bridge, they are rescued by an American helicopter, but Steven unfortunately falls into the water, immediately followed by Mike who leaps to save him, instead Nick is held back by the crew of the aircraft. In the fall, Steven breaks both legs and Mike loads him on his shoulders, until they meet other soldiers and refugees on their way to Saigon, managing to make his friend rest on the hood of a Jeep.

Nick is hospitalized in a military hospital and once discharged, he wanders in the hellish and confusing city of Saigon, among drugs, infamous clubs and prostitutes.

NICK: (Addressing the prostitute) No! I can't stay here in a room with a kid crying. (*The Deer Hunter*, 1978)

Vilmos Zsigmond's exceptional photography beautifully contrasts the horror of death, of the dark Vietnamese hell, of the dark, dirty, chaotic and violent Saigon with previous hunting scenes in a landscape bathed in light, in the blissful and unspoiled nature, in a mystical condition of lightheartedness, happiness, euphoria and even superficiality, as in a sort of Earthly Paradise. From the cool springs of the mountain, which symbolize the place of revelation in mythology, one sinks into the stagnant waters of the Mekong River, into the reed cages in which prisoners are trapped. Even the music plays a fundamental role: they are never used in the most bloody and violent scenes, but are used only in the most reflective and melancholic moments, as in the famous case of the "Cavatina" composed by Stanley Myers.

As he wanders around Saigon, Nick hears gunshots in a building and immediately senses what is happening inside. He would like to get away, but a French businessman named Julien convinces him to come in and play Russian roulette for him. In the restaurant there is also Mike who recognizes his friend Nick, but cannot reach him. Mike then goes home, but it will never be the same again.

Eccovi un uomo
uniforme

Eccovi un'anima
deserta
uno specchio impassibile

(…)
Il raro bene che mi nasce
così piano mi nasce

E quando ha durato
così insensibilmente s'è spento.

Here is a man

uniform

Here is a soul

deserted

an impassive mirror

(...)

The rare good that is born to me

so slowly it is born to me

And when it lasted

so insensibly he died.

(Locvizza, 24 Settembre 1916, "Distacco" in
Il Porto Sepolto di Giuseppe Ungaretti)

Michael, the leader of the group, the strongest, has no physical problems, however, extremely marked by the war experience, has serious problems of reintegration into society and carries with him deep emotional traumas.

He does not show up at the party organized by his friends on the occasion of his return and the following morning, after meeting Linda (from whom he learns that Nick has deserted), he runs into friends who reveal to him the bad condition of Angela, who has become mother of a child and plunged into catatonia after the return of Steven, now irremediably disabled.

The friends left at home seem to understand nothing of the war and appear distant, foreign, almost hostile to Mike's eyes. The protagonist's silence, his feeling of alienation, this closure in himself, this apathy, his constant search for silence and his urgent need for solitude are due to the impossibility of communicating an experience so unacceptable that, at the same time, turns out to be an incomprehensible experience for those who stayed home.

Later Mike, during a hunt, fails to shoot a deer, despite him having it targeted. The deer, like life, manifests itself in a luminous clearing for a few seconds, before disappearing again in the thick of the woods. Surrounded by water, the source of existence, and by light, a symbol of hope, spirit and divinity, Mike, tired of death, chooses life.

This symbolic hunting scene, parallel to that at the beginning of the film, represents a virile ritual closely linked to war which, however, is now rejected by the protagonist, who renounces shooting the game, a sign of the desire for peace and hope part of those who, like him, have returned devastated and marked by this experience.

In the evening, seeing Stanley jokingly threatening Axel with his gun, Mike violently takes it out of his hand and with a single bullet in the drum, points it to his friend's forehead and pulls the trigger, making Stanley understand dangerousness of his gesture. The next day, Mike returns with Linda to the motel where they had spent the night together a few nights earlier, trying to reintegrate into society and the civilized world, and to "get back to normal" through this love affair. Women, however, exist only on the fringes of men's lives.

Steven's mother is a virago, his bride is weak, and the bridesmaids are too much made up and have too many curls, are plump and full of giggles. The only cleverer and deeper woman we see in Clairton is Linda, who works at the supermarket. When Michael returns from Vietnam, his relationships with Linda mostly consist of exchanging unhappy and caring looks. He loves her, but they're lying on a bed together and he, fully clothed, never kisses her, out of respect, as if she's already been promised to his best friend. There is no sex scene in the film, because purity (of the hero), willpower, courage, heroism and friendship are more important here than carnal love between man and woman. Values and ideals are everything to Mike. The protagonist then meets his friend Steven, whose legs have been amputated and who has lost the use of an arm, in a facility for veterans, refusing to go home, even for having learned of Angela's betrayal however, he informs Mike that he periodically receives large sums of money from Vietnam. Mike quickly realizes it is Nick and after forcibly convincing Steven to leave the facility and return to his wife, he returns to Vietnam to find his lost friend.

Wandering through the chaotic and degraded Saigon, in this hellish journey of his, in this catabasis of his, Mike meets Julien and convinces him to take him to the place where he plays Russian roulette, telling him he wants to take part.

The ritual of hunting, as a sacred link between hunter and prey, in the awareness of their profound relationship and in the expectation of a universal life that is eternally renewed only by sacrificing itself to itself, loses any meaning in Russian roulette, becoming an instrument that segregates life in the abysmal abyss of existential emptiness. Mike therefore finds his best friend Nick, who has now become a professional of the terrible game. Nick, in his existential descent, in his complete suffering and degeneration, having abandoned everything, leaving behind his girlfriend, his friends and his job, does not recognize Mike. At this point, he decides to make an extreme attempt to reason with Nick: he sits in front of him and recreates the tremendous experience lived in captivity. Nick, however, as if he did not care about anything, appears imperturbable, indifferent, cold, detached and insensitive to the sight of his friend.

La mia vita

è già

così colma

di morte

Da ogni attimo
che mi sorge
m'irride
quella scia
di bene
andato
(…)
Vorrei essere
piccolo e ignaro
avere
i sensi vergini
godere
senz'apprensione
di quest'abisso
che mi cresce
nel cuore.

My life

is already

so full

of death

From every moment

that rises to me

mocks me

that trail

of good

went

(...)

I wish I was

small and oblivious

to have

the virgin senses

to enjoy

without apprehension

of this abyss

that grows me

in the heart.

("Rimorso" di Giuseppe Ungaretti)

During the game, Mike tries to talk to him, evoking past memories in him, before they left for the war, for Vietnam.

```
MIKE: (...) Nicky, you remember the
trees, all the different ways in the
trees. Remember that? Remember? Huh?
The   mountains.   You   remember   all
that?  (The Deer Hunter, 1978)
```

To recall, in the present of the heart and of the feeling, that childhood and that youth, the sweet and pleasant memory of that happy, carefree, blissful and nostalgic past to become aware of oneself again, of one's origin and one's roots, maturing a reflection in the unpleasant and dark present, plunging into the river of time and life to overcome one's doubts and weaknesses, to heal one's traumas and wounds: the memory of Heaven to get out of Hell. To re-emerge from that inner hell that has left indelible scars on the soul. Nick loved trees, he was amazed by their so different shapes, in which nature, in absolute peace, manifested his creative power.

But, after having fallen into the abyss, he can no longer emerge, the memory of that damned infernal vision blinds him and distracts him from heavenly memories: Nick has lost his love for nature and for its different forms, and for light no longer lights up his face.

This is why he does not want to go home and continues to play with death every night in the clandestine clubs, pointing a gun to his head and pulling the trigger.

Mike ventures into the infamous streets of Saigon to keep his promise made with Nick that night, when life was still quiet and festive. But it's all in vain: Nick, despite having recognized Mike, pulls the trigger and dies right in front of his eyes.

NICK: One shot. (*The Deer Hunter*, 1978)

Memories are not enough, Nick was so shocked by the traumatizing experiences he had in Vietnam that, with his total dissatisfaction, his extreme unhappiness and his existential pessimism, he became irretrievable. He is lost forever.

Death becomes the only way he manages to free himself from the horrors of war. Russian roulette, the representation, according to

Cimino, of the Vietnam War, a useless, absurd and violent game, imposed from above and based on money, a spiritual and psychological cruelty that leads to physical destruction, a perverse hallucination in a world without sense that it has lost love and human dignity, here sadly becomes the only solution to redeem oneself from the atrocities, pain and suffering of conflict. The film begins with a marriage (a union that glorifies love and therefore future life) and ends with a funeral (the celebration of death). All the friends go to Nick's funeral and during the reception in John's bar, in dramatic silence: despite all the suffering suffered, in the throes of emotion, they sing *God bless America*, in honor of their deceased friend. A disheartened hymn backwards, an expression of the pain of a people in the face of the tragedy of war, the self-destructive torment of the USA, but also the proud desire to resume the journey: Nick's duel at Russian roulette is a challenge with himself and with the enemy, it is a struggle with one's own dark side and with that of American society. However, in the chaos of war, friendship, the light of the world, the driving mechanism of existence, an essential bond to resist and continue to fight against adversity, is also expressed beyond the film. John Cazale, who played Stanley in the film, was very ill and in fact, unfortunately, died at the age of forty-two, after filming ended, and since the insurance did not cover his role and the production had refused to pay this exorbitant amount (among other things, following the threats of dismissal addressed to Cazale, Cimino and Meryl Streep threatened to leave the set), Robert De Niro, a friend of John, paid this allowance out of his own pocket to allow him to shoot the part and allow him to fulfill this wish. Unfortunately, however, John was unable to even view the film.

This gesture of solidarity, very beautiful and relevant, beautifully underlines the friendship that pervades the whole film, this absolute bond that unites the protagonists, in which each never abandons the other.

Mike/Robert De Niro cares about everyone and constantly tries to save them, trying to bring them home stubbornly and in every way, even in the awareness of the impossibility of succeeding in any time.

And therefore, whether life endows us with a single blow, with a single possibility, or whether it reserves more blows and opportunities, we must continue to live and fight.

(Operation "Tra Hung Doa" Co "C", 2nd Bn, 27th Inf, 3rd Bde, 25th Inf Div, supported by elements of the 4th Bn, 23rd Inf (Mech), 25th Inf Div, takes part in Operation "Tra Hung Doa," a search and destroy mission. Members of the 1st Plt., Co "C", 2nd Bn, 27th Inf, 3rd Bde, 25th Inf Div, wait for helicopters to arrive and take. 29 February 1968, *Virtual Vietnam Archive*).

God bless America, land that I love
Stand beside her and guide her
Through the night with the light from above

From the mountains to the prairies
To the oceans white with foam
God bless America, my home sweet home

God bless America, land that I love
Stand beside her and guide her
Through the night with the light from above

From the mountains to the prairies
To the oceans white with foam
God bless America, my home sweet home

From the mountains to the prairies
To the oceans white with foam
God bless America, my home sweet home
God bless America, my home sweet home

AUDIOVISUAL AND BIBLIOGRAPHIC SOURCES

All interviews, quotes and dialogues have been partially extracted from the following sources.

Taxi Driver (USA, 1976. Director: Martin Scorsese. Production Co: Bill/Phillips Productions, Italo/Judeo Productions).

The Deer Hunter (USA, United Kingdom, 1978. Director: Michael Cimino. Produced by: Joann Carelli, Michael Cimino, Michael Deeley, John Peverall, Marion Rosenberg, Barry Spikings).

(IMDb movie data, *https://www.imdb.com/* for more details).

BELLITTO R., *Robert De Niro*, Esedra Edizioni, Gallarate, 2001.
RAIMONDI A., RAIMONDI R., *Dove sono finiti i fiori?*, Italy, 2020.
RAIMONDI A., RAIMONDI R., *The Vietnam War Movies*, Italy, 2021.
RAY R. B., *A Certain Tendency of the Hollywood Cinema, 1930-1980*, Princeton University Press, Princeton, New Jersey, 1985.
SLOTKIN R., *Regeneration through Violence: The Mithology of the American Frontier, 1600-1860*, Wesleyan University Press, Middletown, Conn., 1973.

On the cover: *Robert De Niro at 43rd Karlovy Vary International Film Festival*.
Image also usable for commercial purposes, freely modified with a monochromatic platinum effect. From the site: https://commons.wikimedia.org/wiki/File:Robert_De_Niro_KVIFF_portrait.jpg (Author: "Petr Novák, Wikipedia", 5 July 2008). Updated to: 04/01/2021
In p. 88: Photo (public domain, updated to: 04/01/2021) from: https://commons.wikimedia.org/wiki/File:25thInfvietnam1968maskb.jpg
In p. 89, *God Bless America*, National Anthem of the United States of America

As Italian authors, we have done everything possible to ensure that the content of the original work reaches you unaltered in its translation. We apologize for any lexical and morphological errors in the English language. Thanks for your understanding. For any information or other requests you can contact the authors at: *raimondibrothers@gmail.com*

Thank you.

Made in United States
North Haven, CT
20 July 2024

54877405R00055